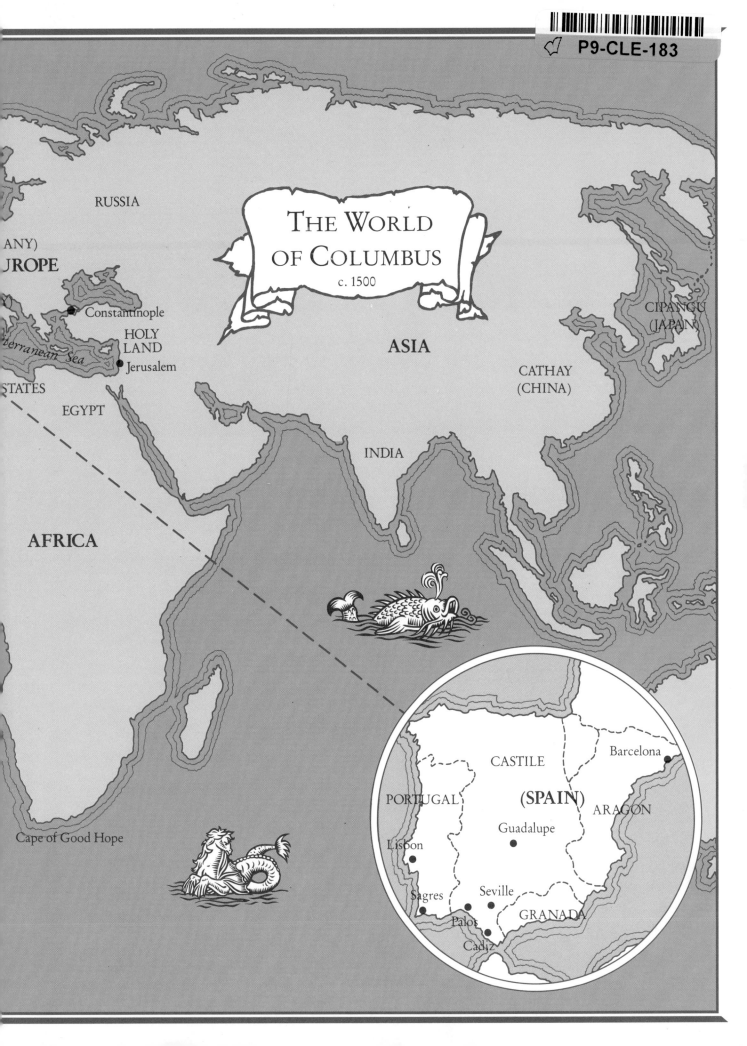

THE VOYAGES OF CHRISTOPHER COLUMBUS

THE VOYAGES OF CHRISTOPHER COLUMBUS

JOHN D. CLARE, Editor

GULLIVER BOOKS
HARCOURT BRACE JOVANOVICH, PUBLISHERS
SAN DIEGO   NEW YORK   LONDON

HBJ

First published in Great Britain in 1992 by The Bodley Head
Children's Books, an imprint of The Random Century Group Ltd

First U.S. edition 1992

Created by Roxby Paintbox Co. Ltd

Library of Congress Cataloging-in-Publication Data
The voyages of Christopher Columbus/John D. Clare, editor. — 1st
U.S. ed.
p.   cm. — (Living history)
Includes index.
"Gulliver books."
Summary: Describes the four voyages of Columbus to the New World
and his activities there.
ISBN 0-15-200507-2
1. Columbus, Christopher — Journeys — America — Juvenile literature.
2. America — Discovery and exploration — Spanish — Juvenile literature.
[1. Columbus, Christopher. 2. Explorers. 3. America — Discovery
and exploration — Spanish.]   I. Clare, John, 1952–   .   II. Series:
Living history (San Diego, Calif.).
E118.V69   1992
970.01′5 — dc20   91-75998

Director of Photography   Tymn Lyntell
Photography   Charles Best
Art Director   Dalia Hartman
Production Manager   Fiona Nicholson
Typesetting   Thompson Type, San Diego, California
Reproduction   Catalyst Repro Technology
Columbia Offset Ltd
Trademasters Ltd

Printed in Hong Kong
A   B   C   D   E

ACKNOWLEDGMENTS

Historical Advisor: Barry Ife, King's College, London. **Makeup:** Alex
Cawrdon, Pam Foster, Stella Jacobs. **Set design and building:** Art FX
Associates, John Preston. **Casting:** Baba Rodgers. **Photographer's
assistants:** Michael Harvey, Nicola Moyes. **Location management**
(Spain): Jacqueline Moya Dixon. **Replica Columbus boats:** Sociedad
Estatal Quinto Centenario. Christopher Columbus portrayed by Manola
Santos.

Additional photographs: Ajax News and Feature Service, pp. 32–33;
Reproduced by permission of the British Library, p. 8, p. 63 top left;
Fotomas Index, p. 43; Hereford Cathedral, p. 6 bottom left; Mansell
Collection, p. 63 bottom right; Mary Evans Picture Library, p. 32; Scala/
Museo Navale di Pegli, p. 62; National Maritime Museum, pp. 44–45;
Sonia Halliday and Laura Lushington Photographs, p. 7 bottom left; Susan
Griggs Agency, pp. 26–27.

Contents

The World of Columbus

Christopher Columbus, one of the most famous explorers in history, was born in Italy halfway through the 15th century, at the end of the time known as the Middle Ages. The Hundred Years' War between France and England had not yet ended, and Johann Gutenberg was still perfecting the printing press.

Europeans of the time knew much less than we do now about science, geography, and the other peoples of the world. Most scholars believed the earth was round, but the *mappae mundi* (world maps drawn up by the Christian Church) still showed a flat earth with Jerusalem at the center.

The Church also argued that if antipodes (people who lived on the other side of the world) existed, they must be the devil's creation, or else they would fall off into space.

A few Europeans, such as Marco Polo, had traveled into Asia and Africa, but their books often mixed fact with fantasy. Writers described man-creatures with ears like elephants, or faces on their chests; others were said to have one huge foot that they held up like an umbrella in the rain. An English traveler, Sir John Mandeville, claimed to have seen the Earthly Paradise — the Garden of Eden — surrounded by mountains, deserts, and rushing rivers. Other tales told of Prester John, a Christian king living somewhere in Africa, who had great wealth and invincible armies. Parts of the Ocean Sea (the Atlantic) were said to be so hot that the water boiled, the tides so strong that a ship that sailed there would never return. Most people had no way to check whether these stories were true or false, and many believed them.

Until 1492 no Europeans knew of the American continents' existence. Scholars thought that to the west, between Europe and Cathay (China), lay one huge ocean in

which sat some large islands they called Brazil, Antilia, and Cipangu (Japan).

Despite all this, the century following 1450 came to be known as the Renaissance, from the French word meaning "rebirth." It seemed that after centuries of stagnation progress had started again. A French writer boasted, "The world sailed around, America discovered, the compass invented, the printing press sowing knowledge, ancient manuscripts rescued, and learning restored: all witness the triumph of our New Age." Columbus, who became known as the "discoverer" of America, played a major part in bringing this new age about.

CHRISTIANS, MUSLIMS, AND MEDITERRANEAN TRADE

During the Renaissance, men dominated public life. Women usually were responsible for the house, farm work, and children, while men ran the government, fought wars, traded, and traveled. Many Renaissance men were violent and arrogant, hoping that if they worked hard enough they could become rich and famous — and change the world.

Catholicism was the official religion of all European countries. People of other religions, even Christians from sects that differed just slightly from Catholicism, were considered heathens who should be conquered and converted. For many years, European armies had been fighting with Muslims for control of the land around the Mediterranean, and during the 15th century the Christians suffered several defeats. Jerusalem and the Holy Land were already in Muslim hands. In 1453 the Turks, who were Muslims, took Constantinople (Istanbul). In 1480 they captured the port of Otranto in Italy and set up a market where they sold Christian slaves. Only in Spain (at that time divided into a number of

states) were Christians able to gain any victories against Muslims. There the Christian rulers of Castile and Aragon conquered the Muslim kingdom of Granada.

In the Middle Ages and early Renaissance, the countries of western Europe imported silk and spices from Asia. Silk was a luxury, but spices that disguised the tastes of bad meat and rotten vegetables were considered essential. By conquering the entire eastern Mediterranean, the Muslims cut Europe off from trade with India and the Far East.

Some Europeans tried to find alternative trade routes to the East. The rulers of Portugal, for example, encouraged voyages of exploration around the south of Africa. They also hoped to discover the kingdom of Prester John so they could make an alliance with him against the Muslims.

Columbus's voyage of 1492 was also intended to discover a route to India and the East — by sailing west, across the Ocean Sea.

THE "NEW WORLD"

The American continents were called the "New World" in Europe, but Columbus was not the first person to reach them. In prehistoric times, tribes from Asia made their way into the continents, probably through Alaska. Ancient Egyptians may also have reached South America; the 20th-century adventurer Thor Heyerdahl sailed a papyrus boat across the Atlantic to prove that it is possible to do so. An inscription, supposedly 2,500 years old, was discovered in Brazil in 1872: "We came from the Red Sea around [Africa] but were separated by a storm," it reads, "so we have come here, 12 men and 3 women." Although this inscription was initially dismissed as a fake because of mistakes in its grammar, scholars have since discovered ancient texts from the Middle East written in exactly the same style. Archaeologists have proved with absolute certainty that, in about A.D. 1000, the Vikings settled in Newfoundland and traded with the native peoples.

During the 1470s and 1480s the Portuguese made a number of attempts to cross the Atlantic, and Danish fishermen sailed beyond Iceland toward Greenland and Labrador. At about the same time, English explorers set out from the port of Bristol to look for the "isle of Brazil." Some historians claim that the English reached Newfoundland in 1481 but kept their discovery a secret while they fished there for cod.

Genoa

Historians are almost certain that Cristoforo Colombo (Christopher Columbus) was born in the Italian port city of Genoa in 1451. They believe he was the son of Domenico Colombo, a wool weaver.

In the 15th century, Italy was divided into small states organized around cities. Genoa was one of the greatest of these city-states. More than 5,000 houses, each five or six stories high, were packed into about half a square mile (130 hectares) inside the city walls. Outside, there were about 2,000 houses, including the mansions of the nobility and wealthy merchants.

Genoa was a prosperous trading center where Christian and Jewish traders from France, Germany, England, Spain, and Portugal, as well as Arabs from Africa, haggled over goods that Genoese merchants had brought from the East. Because of this international trade and several plague epidemics, political feuds, and workers' rebellions, Genoa was an exciting — though dangerous — place to live.

A busy street in Genoa. Below: the city in the 15th century, drawn by an artist of the time.

Sailing and Navigation

Despite the dangers of storms and pirates, the easiest and safest way to travel in the 15th century was by sea. Traders journeying by sea avoided moors and forests, robbers, and wild animals. Genoese ships regularly sailed out into the Atlantic through the Strait of Gibraltar. Portuguese sailors explored the coast of Africa, and in 1487 Bartolomeo Diaz, a Portuguese captain, reached Africa's southern tip, the Cape of Good Hope.

By the 15th century, Europeans had precise charts showing distances and compass bearings for these places. Many historians believe that the Portuguese established a school of navigation at Sagres in midcentury. By the 1490s many sailors had the skills to travel across familiar waters using the sun and the stars for guidance.

Genoa was famous for its mapmakers, traders, and explorers, and many of the city's young men became sailors. Late in his life, Columbus wrote that he went to sea at the age of 14. Few records of the voyages he made in his early years remain, but some evidence suggests that he may have sailed with a pirate called Columbo the Younger.

In 1476 a Genoese ship on which Columbus was a sailor was attacked and sunk off the coast of Portugal. Using an oar to stay afloat, Columbus swam 6 miles (10 kilometers) to land. There he told the Portuguese that he was from a noble family ruined by war. He changed his name to Christovão Colom and eventually married the daughter of a Portuguese nobleman.

Young Genoese boys learn practical seamanship while making local trading and fishing trips along the coast. They study the tides and weather and learn to interpret signs such as floating plants and driftwood.

The Portuguese Experts

When Columbus arrived in 1476, Portugal was at the forefront of Atlantic exploration. There Columbus learned astronomy and arithmetic, and read (as he put it) "everything that has been written" about geography and history. Columbus was not the first person to realize the earth is a sphere or to consider traveling to the East by sailing west around the world. Two hundred years earlier, for example, a Genoese merchant family, the Vivaldis, had tried unsuccessfully to sail to India across the Ocean Sea (the Atlantic).

When Columbus sailed to Africa, he saw that the lands beyond Europe were inhabitable. In Madeira and the Canary Islands, he found unknown plants that had drifted in from the west, and in Britain, he heard stories of strange men who had washed ashore in Ireland. In 1477 Columbus himself sailed 100 leagues — more than 300 miles (480 kilometers) — beyond Iceland.

In 1481 he corresponded with an Italian scholar who had calculated that Cipangu (Japan) was only 3,500 miles (5,600 kilometers) away across the Atlantic. Columbus recalculated the figure to 2,750 miles (4,400 kilometers), and in 1484 he asked King João II of Portugal to finance an expedition across the Ocean Sea to Cipangu.

A group of Portuguese experts in mathematics and geography, called together by King João, question Columbus. He explains his ideas, using dividers.

Cartographers have accurately mapped the coasts of Europe on sea charts called portolans. *Beyond Europe, however, Columbus's charts are guesswork. He has made many mistakes, and the experts reject his calculations. They doubt that Cipangu exists and think he is asking too great a reward.*

Japan is actually more than 12,000 miles (19,300 kilometers) to the west of Portugal. It is sheer chance that the West Indies lie roughly where Columbus estimates Cipangu to be.

La Rábida

I n 1485 Columbus left Portugal an impoverished widower. With his young son, Diego, he traveled to Spain. According to legend, he was so poor that he had to beg for bread and a cup of water from the monastery of La Rábida near the port of Palos.

At La Rábida Columbus met Antonio de Marchena, an influential friar. Marchena arranged for him to meet King Fernando of Aragon and Queen Isabela of Castile (Ferdinand and Isabella), who together ruled Spain, in May 1486. Again Columbus was able to ask a sovereign to sponsor his expedition.

Some historians believe that the queen was intrigued by Columbus, but she referred the matter to a commission led by one of her priests, Hernando de Talavera. For four years Cristóbal Colón, as the Spanish knew him, attended this commission, arguing with churchmen who quoted the Old Testament and the writings of St. Augustine to convince him his proposed voyage would fail. Columbus was a self-taught sailor, and the Spanish scholars treated him with contempt. Meanwhile, he made a living by selling books. He also had a son, Fernando, with a Spanish woman.

In 1490 the Talavera commission reported that Columbus's ideas were "vain and worthy of rejection." It stated that a voyage to Asia would take three years, that St. Augustine had said there were no antipodes, that the places Columbus wanted to visit were uninhabitable, and that a ship that sailed there would never return.

In 1491 Columbus and his son Diego return to La Rábida. One of the friars, Juan Pérez, introduces him to Dr. Fernández, an astronomer; Pero Vásquez, an experienced navigator; and Martín Alonso Pinzón, a local merchant and sea captain. As Diego watches, they help Columbus to rethink his arguments. In July 1491 the little group decides to approach the king and queen once again.

Encamped Outside Granada

Many people in Renaissance Europe feared the world was going to end in 1500. There were rumors that in Germany the rain had turned to blood and that in Rome a bolt of lightning had thrown the Pope from his throne. Many people turned to religion for comfort, hoping to appease God and convince him to spare the world.

In Spain, Isabela shared this religious devotion. Believing that Catholicism was the only true religion, Isabela herself donned full armor to lead a war against the Muslim kingdom of Granada (whose capital city was also called Granada). During her reign more than 150,000 Jews living in Spain were expelled. Together she and Fernando introduced the Inquisition to hunt down Spanish heretics (people whose religious beliefs were not strictly in line with Catholic teachings). A suspected heretic could be called in, questioned, and tortured to extract a confession. Convicted heretics were most often executed. More than 10,000 "heretics" were burned at the stake.

One historian has suggested that Columbus was a Jew hoping to find a new world where Jews could go to escape from Isabela. But evidence shows Columbus supported the queen's religious fanaticism. According to one writer of the time, he fought "with distinguished bravery" at Granada and offered to use the profits of his expedition to the Indies for a crusade to reconquer Jerusalem from the Muslims.

The sovereigns' conquest of Granada (January 1492) financially frees them to support Columbus. As he kneels before them, they order him to sail westward to reach India, appointing him Admiral of the Ocean Sea and Governor of the Indies, and promising him a tenth of the wealth of the lands he finds. They will pay a generous annuity — 10,000 maravedis, or about 70 dollars — to the person who first sights land.

Equipping the First Voyage

Columbus, now Admiral of the Ocean Sea, returned to Palos on May 22, 1492, with letters from Fernando and Isabela ordering the town to supply and equip ships for his voyage within ten days.

He met with a cool reception. According to an eyewitness, "the inhabitants of Palos thought that anyone who sailed with Columbus was death-marked." They complained about the trouble of organizing an expedition already rejected by the Portuguese.

When Martín Alonso Pinzón set about recruiting men for Columbus, he met with more success. It was said that "for every man he had pleasant words and money; so that with this and the general trust in him, many people followed him." When ten weeks had elapsed, everything was ready for the expedition.

Columbus's fleet comprised three tiny ships. The *Niña* and the *Pinta* were caravels, fast and sturdy ships developed by the Portuguese for their voyages of exploration. To Columbus's annoyance, his third ship, the *Santa María*, was a *nao*, a heavy cargo ship that rolled around in the sea like a barrel. All three ships were smaller than 100 tons (a 100-ton ship could carry 100 tuns, or barrels, of wine); none was longer than 80 feet (24 meters).

Martín Alonso Pinzón, Columbus, and the ship's chandler supervise the loading of food and equipment. Careful records must be kept to show to the sovereigns who are paying for the voyage.

Palos is on Spain's Atlantic coast, and many of the local seamen are experienced sailors. Some have gone on Portuguese expeditions into the Ocean Sea. Others have sailed with the local fishing fleet or accompanied slave traders along the coast of Africa.

Setting Sail

In all, 90 men joined the expedition as crew members. All but 4 of them were Spanish. The king and queen sent a few government officials, including an interpreter, who spoke Arabic, a language that the Spanish thought the people in the Indies would understand. Columbus took charge of the *Santa María*. Martín Alonso Pinzón captained the *Pinta*, and his younger brother Vicente took charge of the *Niña*.

At dawn on August 3, 1492, the three ships set sail. In his log (the record book of the voyage, which he intended to present to Fernando and Isabela), Columbus wrote that he sailed "in the Name of Our Lord, Jesus Christ, . . . to the regions of India, to see the Princes there and the peoples and the lands, and to learn the measures that could be taken for their conversion to our Holy Faith."

On the fourth day at sea the *Pinta*'s rudder broke. All three ships were forced to stop for a month in the Canary Islands while shipwrights repaired the damage. Columbus took the opportunity to have the triangular sails on the *Niña* changed to square rigs like those on the other ships. Triangular sails are better for sailing against the wind, but square sails are faster when, like Columbus, you are sailing with the wind behind you.

The ships set off again on September 6. As the Canaries disappeared from sight and the winds and currents drove the ships westward, the crews may have wondered whether they would ever see their families again.

Columbus sets sail on the same tide as the last ship carrying the Jews who have been expelled from Spain — they are fleeing to Morocco, moving south while he goes west.

On the Voyage

Different crew members had different jobs on Columbus's ships. The pilot was in charge of navigation. He "logged" the ship's speed by dropping a plank in the water and watching how quickly the ship sailed past it. He recorded the ship's direction, as shown on the compass, by inserting a peg into a traverse board every half hour. Then, since he knew both direction and speed, he calculated the ship's position and marked it on a sheepskin chart by pricking the map with his dividers. This method of navigation is called dead reckoning.

Columbus purposely underestimated distances. He thought the crew might panic if they found out how far they had sailed — though because of primitive techniques his "false" estimates were sometimes more accurate than the "true" ones.

The boatswain looked after the sails and anchors, killed rats, and made sure the galley (an iron firebox used for cooking) was safely extinguished at night. The steward supervised food, water, and wine supplies. Below deck, a caulker manned the pumps

and tried to stop leaks. Three doctors, a cooper (who mended barrels), and a gunner also sailed with the fleet.

The helmsman, who is in charge of the rudder, stands in the afterdeck. He cannot see the sky or sails, so the pilot or master (who is in charge of the whole crew) shouts down instructions from the deck. In heavy seas, it takes up to a dozen men to control the rudder.

There are no clocks on board. Throughout the day, a gromet (ordinary seaman) turns the half-hour glass. At night, the sailors also tell time by looking at the stars.

Right, clockwise: A half-hour glass, a compass, an astrolabe (to calculate the ship's position using the stars), a logbook, quill pens, dividers, and (in the center) a traverse board.

Life on Board

Each day was divided into six watches of four hours each. The first watch of the day began at 3 A.M., when a boy sang a short hymn, then said the Lord's Prayer and a short prayer for "good days, good voyage, and good company."

At about 11 A.M. a gromet spread a cloth on deck and laid out some ship's biscuit and beef bones. There might also be some beans, dried meat or fish, and even some wine. All the ship's company, saying "Amen," immediately rushed out and devoured the food. One traveler on a different voyage complained: "It is like an anthill."

The afternoon watch (3–7 P.M.) was fairly easy, and while the lookout kept watch the men were able to do routine maintenance, such as splicing ropes and mending sails. Some told tales and searched for lice in their clothes and hair. At sunset a boy sang the *Salve Regina*, a hymn to the Virgin Mary.

Below: Columbus and the captains have cabins, but the sailors sleep on deck; their favorite places are the flat hatch covers. There is little furniture on board. A captain takes three chests for his personal belongings, but three gromets have to share one chest. A precarious, wave-battered wooden seat hanging over the handrail serves as the toilet. In bad weather it is rarely used, and sewage collects in chamberpots in the hold.
Far right: A gromet climbs up the "ratlines" to adjust the rigging and the sails.
Top right: Examining the lead. A plumb-line is used to test the depth of the water. Fat is smeared on the bottom to reveal the nature of the seabed; the sand, shells, or stone stick to the fat.
Center right: The sailors' diet includes neither fruit nor vegetables. Many men die of scurvy, a disease caused by lack of vitamin C.
Below right: A sailor splices two pieces of rope, joining them together.

First Sighting

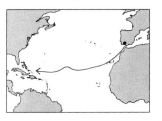

By October 6 the sailors on Columbus's ships were growing restless. Many historians believe that the *Santa María*'s crew, worried that they would never reach land, were openly threatening to throw Columbus overboard and return home. According to this story, Martín Alonso Pinzón shouted from his ship that he would hang the troublemakers if the Admiral wished. There was no more talk of mutiny that day.

Around this time, lookouts had begun to spot signs that land was near, and a few false claims to land sightings were made, but Columbus refused to turn off course to investigate. Instead, he warned that anyone mistakenly crying "Land!" would forfeit the prize offered for the first sighting.

On October 11, 1492, lookouts saw a carved stick and a twig covered in barnacles

floating in the sea. Thinking that land was near, Columbus doubled the number of lookouts. He did not want his voyage to end in shipwreck on an unknown reef. Standing on deck at about midnight, Columbus thought he saw a light "like a little wax candle." At 2 A.M. on October 12, gunfire from the *Pinta* told him that land had been sighted.

Columbus anchored off one of a group of islands known today as the Bahamas. He went ashore, planted the royal banner, took possession of the territory in the name of the king and queen of Spain, and called it San Salvador, meaning "Holy Savior." He also named two nearby islands Fernandina and Isabela after the Spanish sovereigns. Although he later called the lands he had reached an *otro mundo* (other world), at first Columbus thought he had reached Asia.

It is 2 A.M. on October 12, 1492. Rodrigo de Triana, the lookout on the Pinta, *sights land. Columbus promises Rodrigo the reward that Fernando and Isabela have offered, but later he will claim the prize for himself, insisting that he had seen the fires of the island first.*

The Taino People

The tiny island Columbus named San Salvador was home to a people who called themselves Tainos. They must have been surprised when a large wooden boat landed and strangely dressed men got out.

Columbus reported that the Tainos lived a peaceful, unhurried life, and that most of their leisure time was spent lying in *hamaca* (hammocks), smoking dried leaves called *tabaca* through Y-shaped tubes while the older women told stories.

Among the Tainos, old people cared for the children and prepared the meals. Everyone ate sweet potatoes (called *batata*, from which comes our word "potato"), and bread made from the cassava root.

The young women cultivated the fields and the young men hunted for snakes, turtles, and iguanas (which were considered a great delicacy). The Tainos used the *guacicomo* (a species of fish with suckers around its mouth) to catch other fish. When it attached itself to its prey, the fishermen hauled them both in by means of a string fastened through the *guacicomo*'s tail.

The Tainos worshiped a supreme god but also believed in lesser *zemi*s (spirits) and the power of curses. Some families kept an ancestor's skull in a small basket, thinking the ancestor's spirit would protect them. These friendly and gentle people delighted Columbus, who believed they thought he and his men were gods. "They love their neighbor as themselves . . . and always speak with a smile," he wrote. Several Tainos learned Spanish and served as interpreters. The Spaniards felt safe among them, for as Columbus estimated, "fifty armed men will make them do everything we want."

Led by their cacique (chief), the native people trade and exchange gifts with the Spaniards. They are Lucayans of the Caribbean Taino culture, but, believing he is in the Indies, Columbus calls them Indios *(Indians).*

Shipwrecked at La Navidad

Over the next month the Spaniards sailed from island to island, exploring the region. On November 22, Martín Alonso Pinzón deserted, sailing off in the *Pinta* to look for an island of gold that the native people had told him about. "It was a dirty trick," Columbus wrote in his log.

On December 6, Columbus came upon the land we now call Haiti and marveled at its "beauty and excellence." It so reminded him of home that he named it La Isla Española (the Spanish island).

On Christmas Eve, 1492, Columbus set sail along the north coast of Española. He left the deck at 11 P.M. The helmsman slipped away to sleep, leaving only a young gromet to turn the glass and hold the tiller. As the boy turned the second half hour of the watch, the ship ran aground.

Like most ships of the time, the *Santa María* was fastened together with wooden pegs. She literally fell apart, and Columbus was forced to abandon ship. The crew salvaged what they could. The local cacique, Guacangarí, gave his shipwrecked visitors two large houses in the center of his village. He also gave them gold and jewelry.

Columbus left 39 of his men, including a doctor, a carpenter, and a gunner, to found a colony in this friendly place. He called the settlement La Navidad (Nativity) because the shipwreck occurred on Christmas Day. He ordered his men to build a fort from the timbers of the *Santa María* and then to look for gold.

These Spanish gunners give an artillery display to impress the Tainos. "It is right," Columbus writes in his log, "that the Indians may obey Your Highnesses with love and fear."

Home to Palos

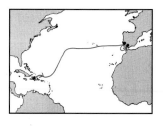

On January 4, 1493, Columbus and most of his men left La Navidad, heading for Spain in the *Niña*. With them they took a small group of Tainos. Two days later, the *Niña* met the *Pinta* off the coast of Española. Columbus wrote that he and Martín Alonso Pinzón exchanged no harsh words, avoiding conflict in order "to prevent Satan from hindering this voyage." Back in La Navidad, the sailors who had stayed behind had already stopped work on the fort, seeing little to fear from the Tainos.

The two ships steered north and caught the westerly trade winds across the Atlantic. They sailed slowly because the *Pinta*'s mast was rotting and both vessels were suffering from shipworm. For three days (February 12–14), they endured a violent storm. Both ships survived, but they were separated.

On March 4, 1493, the *Niña* sailed into Lisbon, Portugal's capital. For a week Columbus stayed there and boasted about his success to King João II, infuriating the Portuguese courtiers. Meanwhile, the *Pinta* had reached northern Spain.

On Friday, March 15, both the *Niña* and the *Pinta* returned to their home port of Palos. The *Pinta*'s crew had been the first to sight land in the New World, and they were the first to arrive in Spain with the news, but it was Columbus who received the most praise. Martín Alonso Pinzón, who had fallen ill, died a few days later.

As the storm drives the Pinta *from view, the sailors of the* Niña *fear they will die, perhaps devoured by a sea monster (below). Columbus is afraid he will not survive to tell anybody about his voyage. When they draw lots to see who will go on pilgrimage if they are saved, Columbus picks the marked bean.*

Processions and Praise

Columbus rested for a fortnight at La Rábida, then set off on the long journey to Barcelona to meet the sovereigns.

Columbus was not the first person to sail across the Atlantic, but the publicity he arranged for himself helped assure his place in history. At the head of the procession to Barcelona walked the six Tainos who had completed the journey, painted and wearing gold ornaments, followed by men carrying parrots and exotic stuffed animals. Columbus followed on horseback, surrounded by a host of young noblemen begging to go on the next voyage. At every village the people turned out to stare and cheer.

On April 30, 1493, Columbus arrived in Barcelona. The sovereigns conferred their highest honors on him. Before he ate, a servant tasted his food to make sure it was

not poisoned, and Columbus rode in public next to King Fernando, an honor previously given only to the king's son. A popular legend later said that Columbus, insulted at a feast by a man who said that someone else would eventually have discovered the islands, invited the guests to balance an egg on its end. After they had all failed he crushed the end and stood the egg on the table. "Everything is easy," he said, "when someone has shown you what to do."

When Columbus arrives, the sovereigns rise as if receiving a person of the highest rank. They forbid Columbus to kneel to kiss their hands, and instead they invite him to sit in their presence.

Columbus speaks for an hour. He has been to Cipangu, he says, and has brought back gold and jewelry—a sample, he claims, of the wealth of this land, where the rivers run with gold.

He calls the Tainos out from behind a screen and speaks of their gentleness and their willingness to receive the Catholic faith.

While the choir sings a **Te Deum,** *Fernando and Isabela, in tears, fall to their knees and thank God.*

Pilgrimage and Prayers

To Columbus it seemed that his success in reaching the New World was certain proof that God approved of him and his actions. God "grants to all who walk in His way victory over apparent impossibilities," he wrote.

At court, Columbus promised to assemble an army of 4,000 cavalrymen and 50,000 foot soldiers to recapture the Holy Sepulcher at Jerusalem. He had the six Tainos who had traveled to Spain baptized. And he changed his signature again, this time to Christoferens — or "the bearer of Christ." He wrote: "I knew that they were a people to be delivered to our holy faith rather by love than by force."

Columbus never would have the opportunity to go on crusade. Fernando and Isabela immediately gave orders for a second expedition to the New World, the first task of which was to be the conversion of the native peoples. Benedictine monk Bernardo Buil and five priests were to go with the

fleet to perform the baptisms, and Columbus was instructed to treat the Tainos "very well and lovingly."

Above: Columbus's new signature. The three Greek letters at the start of his name stand for "Christo." It is not known what the letters above his name mean, but scholars believe they denote some religious phrase such as "I am the servant of the Most High" or "I will save the Holy Sepulcher."
Right: Columbus, on a pilgrimage, kneels at the shrine of Our Lady of Guadalupe and gives thanks to this protector of sailors. He promises the monks that on his next voyage he will name an island after their village.

The Second Voyage

In 15th-century Europe, it was not thought wrong to conquer other lands and take their riches. Immediately after Columbus's return, Fernando persuaded the Pope to issue a bull (order) "giving" Spain all the lands west of the Atlantic Ocean. This contradicted an earlier bull in which the Pope had granted to Portugal all the land south of the Canary Islands. In 1494, after months of negotiation, Fernando and João II eventually agreed to divide the world between themselves.

While the issue was still in dispute, however, Fernando and Isabela hurried to take control of the lands Columbus had reached. They ordered Juan de Fonseca, archdeacon of Seville, to equip a fleet of 17 ships — Columbus's second voyage was to be the largest colonizing expedition ever made. Fernando and Isabela also gave Columbus secret orders to map as much of the new lands as possible, to further establish Spain's claim to these places.

For Columbus's second voyage, each ship is loaded with tools, tar, sailcloth, salt pork, water, cooking pots, candles, iron fetters, weapons, fishhooks, astronomical almanacs, and hawk bells (to trade with the native peoples). Live cattle, donkeys, pigs, cats, and chickens are also taken aboard. An official of the Inquisition keeps a stern eye on the sailors as they load the supplies of ship's biscuit. The ships carry a two-year supply of wine, but the barrels leak badly and most of it will be lost.

Encouraged by the reports of gold, more than 1,200 men have joined Columbus's second expedition, each expecting to become instantly wealthy. Many sailors from the first voyage have signed up again. Other passengers are noblemen, farmers, and bricklayers, as well as Columbus's brother Diego. There are also many soldiers, including 20 cavalrymen. Their horses are poor, but they will be the first horses in the New World. Two Spanish-speaking Tainos make the voyage, to serve as interpreters.

The Caribs

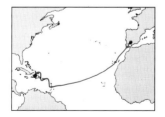

The fleet set sail on September 25, 1493. The weather was fair, except for a storm on October 26, when the sailors saw St. Elmo's fire (lightning running along the mast) and sang hymns of thanks, believing that St. Elmo would save them. On November 3, after a crossing of only 22 days, they sighted land.

Intending to explore some more islands, Columbus had deliberately sailed farther south than in 1492. One of these islands he named Santa María de Guadalupe, as the Spanish monks had requested. There Diego Márquez of Seville, the captain of one of the ships, ignored orders and went ashore. He got lost, and search parties had to go after him.

Guadalupe was covered with a dense forest of sweet-smelling trees and shrubs. The search parties found a fruit they had never seen before, which the native peoples called the *anana* (pineapple). They also claimed to have seen human limbs hung like meat from beams and the body of a young Taino being boiled with geese and parrots. Although Márquez was found unharmed, it seemed to the Spanish who heard these reports that the inhabitants — the Caribs (or Canibs) — were not gentle cowards but fierce, inhu-

man monsters. Historians now believe that the Spanish reports were greatly exaggerated, but the name Carib has given us the word "cannibal," as well as "Carribean."

On November 27 the fleet reached Española. The adventurers found that La Navidad had been destroyed and the men Columbus had left behind were dead.

_____

Eager to amass more wealth, Spanish sailors looking for Márquez have paused to pan for gold. They are alarmed at the sight of Carib warriors.

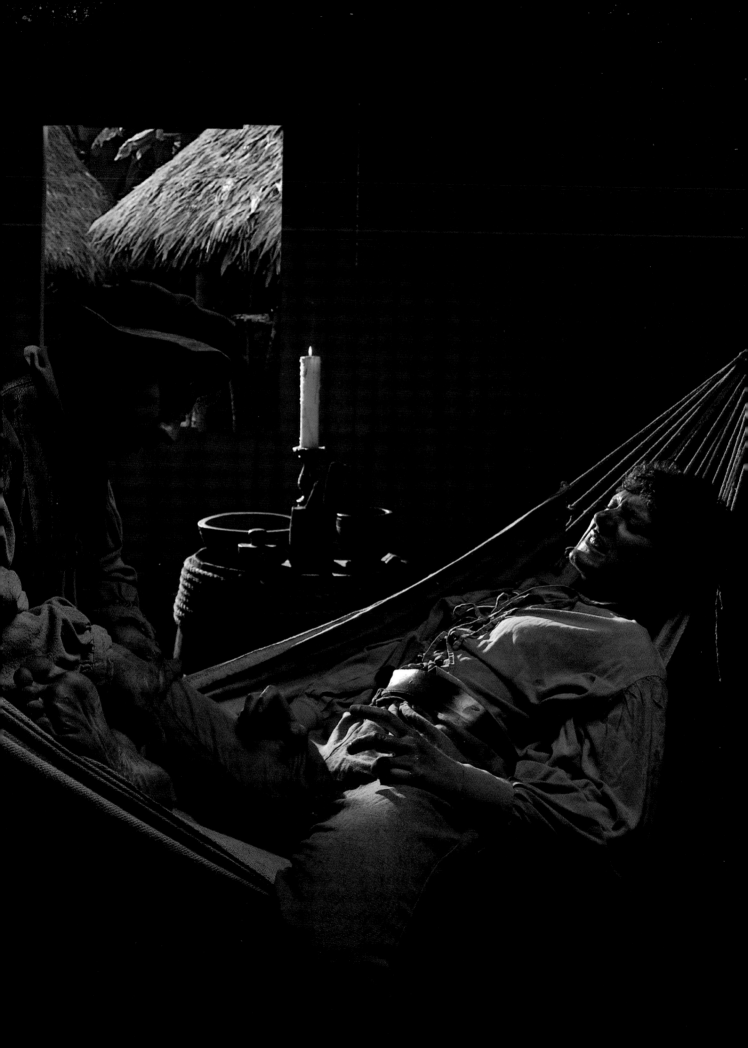

Failure at Isabela

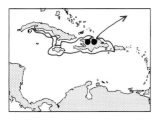

On January 2, 1494, Columbus and his men began to build a town, which Columbus named Isabela. Then, leaving his brother Diego in charge, Columbus set out to explore the coast of Cuba, which he thought might be Cathay (China).

Back on Española, Father Bernardo Buil refused to baptize Tainos until they had learned about Christ. Since the interpreters were away looking for gold, the priests made very few converts. The Spanish nobles and soldiers refused to farm the land. They made slaves of Tainos, forcing them to do the work. Many Tainos were falling sick and dying from European illnesses to which they had no immunity; others committed suicide. When Columbus returned, disappointed that he had not found Cathay, Diego had gone back to Spain, leaving him with an explosive situation. In March 1495, when 10,000 Tainos rebelled, Columbus easily crushed them. In 1494 there were 300,000 Tainos on Española, but 50 years later barely 500 remained. In addition the local environment was badly damaged: European animals devoured native vegetation, and European agricultural methods stripped the soil, making it infertile.

To Isabela and Fernando, Columbus claimed he had found "an incredible amount of gold," but he sent back only a few samples. When the sovereigns sent an official to inspect the colony, Columbus realized his position was in danger. Leaving his newly

arrived brother Bartolomeo in charge, he left for Spain in March 1496.

Isabela is an unhealthy site for a town. The surgeons purge the bowels of the sick and apply leeches to draw the "bad" blood out (left and above), but many colonists die. Although the settlers force Tainos to pan for gold (below), in Spain, people say that the only gold to come out of Española is in the faces of the jaundice victims.

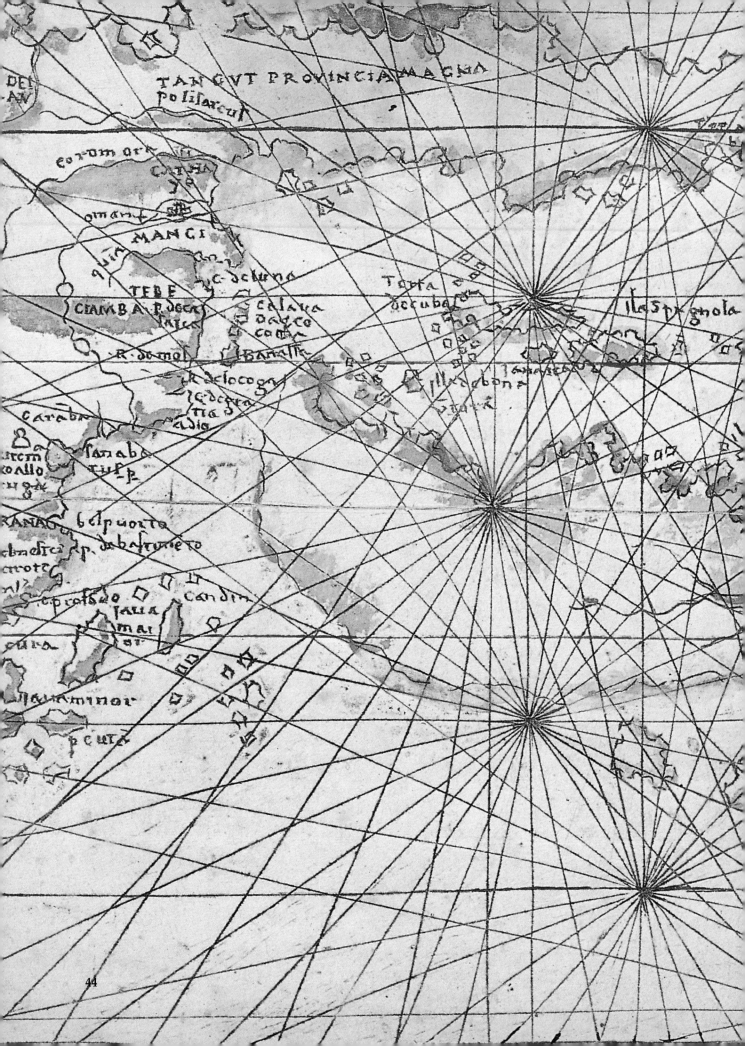

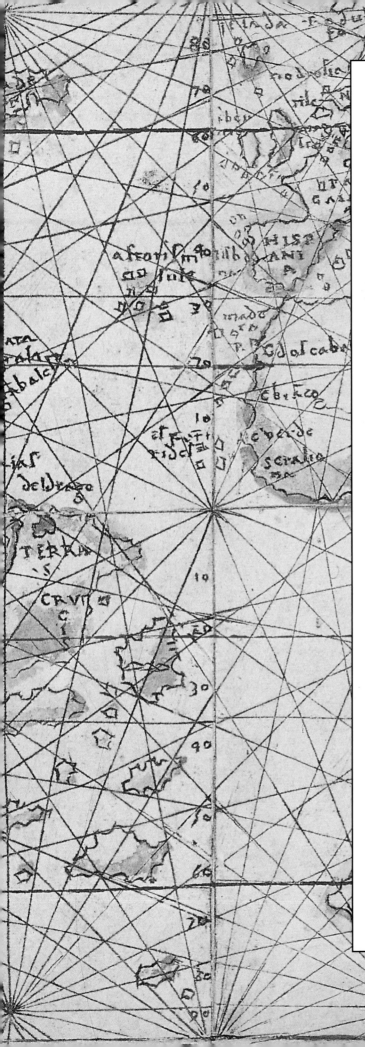

Exploring the New World

In Spain Columbus asked for money and ships to make a third voyage. Isabela and Fernando were reluctant. They were at war with Italy and could not afford the eight ships Columbus requested. Prompted by Bernardo Buil, Spanish priests who saw the Taino statues of *zemis* (spirits) said that the Tainos worshiped the devil. Columbus feared the colony would be abandoned and that he would "see all his work go for nothing." But eventually the Spanish monarchs agreed to give him six ships.

Meanwhile, Giovanni Caboto, an Italian living in England (where he was known as John Cabot), crossed the Atlantic and reached North America in May 1497. In 1498 Vasco da Gama, a Portuguese captain, became the first European to reach India by sea when he sailed south and west around Africa's Cape of Good Hope. Vasco da Gama's voyage took two years.

European explorers reached Brazil in 1500, Florida by 1513, and the Pacific Ocean in 1513. Finally, in 1519, five ships under the command of Fernão de Magalhaes (Ferdinand Magellan), a Portuguese captain in the service of Spain, set off on a voyage around the world.

Columbus's early predictions of civilizations and untold wealth beyond the Atlantic proved to be true, although not in the way he expected. By 1535, Spanish adventurers had reached and destroyed the Aztec empire in Mexico and had conquered the Inca empire in South America. Spain became the superpower of the Western World.

On Francesco Rosselli's sea chart, c. 1508, Hispagnola (Española) and Cuba are accurately drawn, but South America is shown as an island, not a continent, and Cathay (China) is where North America should be.

Exploiting the New World

Europeans were eager to hear about new lands and new trading opportunities. One widely read account of the New World was written by a merchant and explorer from Florence, Amerigo Vespucci. In his account, Amerigo claimed to have sailed across the Atlantic four times and to have been with the first Europeans to reach the mainland — as a result, Europeans called the continent America.

After 1503 trade with the Americas was controlled by the Casa de Contratacion, a new government department in Spain. Explorers and merchants brought back gold and silver from Mexico and Peru, pearls from Venezuela, and brazilwood from Brazil. The fashion-conscious enjoyed American imports when they took snuff, chewed tobacco (which was considered a medicine), and drank chocolate. By the end of the 16th century, corn, which Columbus had brought back from his first voyage, and the potato were common in Europe. America also proved to be a new source of sugar.

By 1550 over 60 ships a year, sailing in convoy to avoid pirates, were sent back to Europe. In return, colonists received everyday essentials such as clothing, wheat, household utensils, and weapons, as well as luxuries such as wine, glass, and books. European traders also supplied colonists with African slaves. The first slaves arrived in America in 1502, and in 1510 the Casa de Contratacion sent 250 black Africans to work in the mines of Española.

The riches of America include many kinds of food as well as gold, cotton, and wood. Clockwise, from top: yams, sugar cane, sweet potatoes, cassava root, cocoa beans, guavas, ginger, gold, cotton, maize, and brazilwood. Center: Tobacco leaves, papayas, and peppers.

The Third Voyage

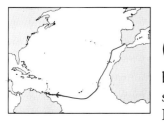

On May 30, 1498, Columbus once again set sail for America. His goal was to investigate reports of a great continent to the south of the Indies, because, as Columbus wrote, people thought that "precious things come from very hot regions where the inhabitants are black." On the way, the fleet was becalmed in the doldrums, waters near the equator where there is little wind. The ships drifted under a blazing sun. "The casks of wine and water burst. The wheat burned like fire; the salt pork scorched and went bad," wrote Columbus — perhaps with some exaggeration, for he was ill during the voyage.

On July 31, when only one barrel of fresh water was left on board Columbus's ship, the summits of three mountains appeared on the horizon. Thanking God for his deliverance, Columbus named the island after the Holy Trinity — La Trinidad.

After taking on fresh water, the fleet sailed south of the island and landed on the Paria peninsula of South America on August 5, 1498. The water was fresh for 72 miles (115 kilometers) from the shore — evidence, Columbus concluded, of a huge river (the Orinoco) flowing into the sea. Where there is a large river, there must be a large mass of land. "This land is a great continent, unknown until now," he wrote.

For the first time, Europeans stood on the South American mainland.

To calculate latitude, Columbus estimates how far the stars are above the horizon; since the earth's surface is curved, the stars' height appears to change according to the latitude from which they are observed. He uses a quadrant (left and below) to measure the angle of altitude, which a gromet reads off the scale on the bottom.

Sometimes a navigator might use a cross staff (above), adjusting the transom (crosspiece) to determine the height of the star.

On his first voyage, Columbus noticed that magnetic north — the direction in which the compass needle points — changed as he crossed the Atlantic. Now, on Paria, he checks his calculations, with the same result. He decides that the earth's shape "is not a true sphere, as scholars have told us, but more like that of a pear" and that he is now near "the stalk, where it sticks out." On top of this mountain, he believes, is the Earthly Paradise, the Garden of Eden.

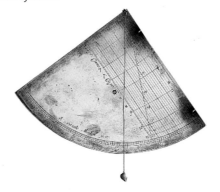

Rebellion and Imprisonment

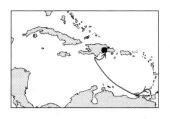

By mid-August 1498 Columbus was very ill. His eyes were so sore that they bled, and he was forced to call off his explorations. He sailed to Española.

The Spaniards' conditions on Española had improved. Bartolomeo and Diego (who had returned) had moved the colonists from Isabela to a healthier site on the south coast of Española. They called it Santo Domingo, after their father, Domenico. The colony was producing bread, pork, and beef. In October they sent a boatload of Taino slaves and brazilwood to Spain.

The Taino caciques were still at war with the Spaniards, however, and many colonists, led by Francisco Roldán, the *alcalde* (chief justice) of the settlement, were also in revolt.

After 13 months Columbus gave in to the *alcalde*, letting him keep his title and permitting the rebels to return to Spain. But when a man abducted Roldán's Taino mistress, the *alcalde* caused another revolt by imprisoning the man. This time the rebels were defeated, and when their leader, Adrian de Moxica, refused to say confession to a priest, Columbus had him thrown from the prison walls.

Back in Spain, angry ex-colonists told Fernando and Isabela that Columbus was a cruel man, a "shedder of Spanish blood," who planned to make himself king of the New World. In 1500 the sovereigns sent Francisco de Bobadilla to see what was going on. He arrested the Columbus brothers and sent them back to Spain in chains.

Columbus's men have overcome a small group of rebels. Many criminals were let out of prison to supply the third voyage's need for volunteers, and a large number of former convicts have joined the revolt. Today, the defeated rebels will be hanged on the spot.

Columbus in Chains

Chains still bound Columbus when he arrived in Spain in October 1500. Accompanied by his jailer, he went to stay at the monastery of Las Cuevas in Seville. "I have made a new voyage, to a new heaven and a new earth, and made Spain the wealthiest of countries," he complained, "yet I am treated as if I had stolen the Indies. Who would believe such a thing?"

While Columbus was at Las Cuevas he rested, prayed, and wrote two books. In *The Book of Privileges* he collected all the documents showing what rights and titles the sovereigns had promised him. *The Book of Prophecies* included a number of biblical passages that he used to support his argument that God had chosen him to discover the route to the Indies.

Two months later, the sovereigns received Columbus at court. His chains were removed, but Fernando and Isabela would not commit to reinstating Columbus as Governor of the Indies. In September 1501, Nicolás de Ovando, one of Fernando's favorites, was appointed to the office. Ovando set sail in February 1502 with 30 ships and 2,500 men. For the rest of his life, Columbus would keep the chains in his bedroom to remind himself of how he had been repaid for his services.

Not long after Ovando sailed, on March 14, 1502, Fernando and Isabela did authorize a fourth Atlantic voyage for Columbus. On this voyage, as on his first voyage, they instructed him to seek a westward sea passage to India.

On his way to meet Fernando and Isabela in December 1500, Columbus refuses to remove his shackles. He has been put in chains in the sovereigns' names, he says, and only the sovereigns can remove them.

When crowds along the route see how he has been treated, there is a public outcry. To them, he is still a hero.

The Fourth Voyage

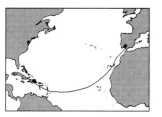

Columbus was 51 years old when, on May 9, 1502, he set out from Cadiz with 4 ships for his fourth voyage. With him went his 12-year-old son, Fernando (who wrote an account of the voyage many years later), and his brother Bartolomeo. The crew — 56 ship's boys and 43 ordinary seamen — was made up of old friends from past voyages and young boys looking for adventure.

The ships had an easy voyage to the Indies, arriving at Matininó (Martinique) on June 15. Then, against the sovereigns' clear orders, Columbus sailed to Española. He wanted to exchange one of his ships, the *Santiago,* which was "a crank and a dull sailer," for a better vessel. In addition, he had noticed a number of dolphins and seals, and deduced from their sudden appearance that a storm was about to break.

At Santo Domingo, however, Nicolás de Ovando refused to allow Columbus's ships to enter the harbor. Ovando had spent three months sorting out the problems Columbus had been unable to solve. Bobadilla was about to return to Spain with a fleet of 28 ships, a large amount of gold, and most of the rebels, and Ovando did not want Columbus causing trouble. As to the storm, the Spaniards at Santo Domingo openly mocked the Admiral as "a prophet and a fortune-teller." While Columbus's 4 ships found shelter in a nearby bay, Bobadilla's fleet set sail for Spain.

Before Columbus sets off on his fourth voyage he refits his ships. After scraping the barnacles off the ships' bottoms, his men repair the caulking (waterproofing), using a hemp rope and tar. The hulls will then be covered with tallow (animal fat).

Seeking a Westward Passage

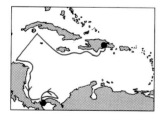

On June 30, 1502, the storm Columbus had predicted struck. Bobadilla and the rebels drowned, and 24 ships sank immediately. Columbus and his men, safe in harbor, survived the storm. When the weather cleared, they sailed westward, exploring the coast of Central America, looking for a westward passage to India.

The native inhabitants on the mainland were experts at weaving cotton shawls and working copper, but according to Columbus's son Fernando they were "painted like devils" and thought the Spaniards were trying to bewitch them. On October 17, at Guayaga, a group of native people attacked the ships, blowing horns and spitting at the Spaniards — a type of curse. Fernando

wrote that on November 9, when Columbus tried to capture some of them, they swam away from his boats, diving like sea birds and easily escaping capture.

The bad weather returned. Columbus fell ill with gout. Finally, on January 6, 1503, the fleet moored in the mouth of a river that Columbus called the Belén (Bethlehem). They built a small settlement. Rain fell ceaselessly until February 14, and the ships became trapped by a sandbank that formed in the river mouth. The inhabitants of this area, which Columbus named Veragua (present-day Panama), told him that there was sea on both sides of the land and that it was just ten days' sail to India. The fleet was only a few miles from the Pacific Ocean, but it was still thousands of miles away from the passage to India.

The Tainos of Española call the storm of June 30 a huracán. *Only one of Bobadilla's ships manages to reach Spain safely. It is the one carrying Columbus's share of the gold mined in the past year. To Columbus, the storm is God's judgment. To his enemies, it seems like witchcraft.*

Jamaica Moon

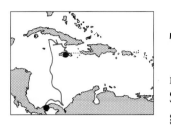

The native people did not want the Spaniards in Veragua. In March 1503 Columbus learned that the *Quibián* (local chief) intended to massacre him and his men. The Spaniards abandoned their new settlement and one ship still trapped inside the sandbar, and set sail for Española in the three remaining vessels.

By now the ships were full of wormholes, and one of them finally sank. The two that remained made it to Jamaica. On June 25 the men ran them aground, fortified them, and used palm leaves to make shelters on the decks.

There was no hope that they would be rescued by a passing ship. Columbus bought two Taino canoes and ordered

Diego Méndez, his chief clerk, and Bartholomeo Fieschi, a sailor from Genoa, to paddle to Española — a journey of more than 100 miles (160 kilometers). Then he waited, trading hawks' bells and sailors' caps for cassava bread and meat.

By February the Tainos had tired of trading food for trinkets. On the 29th, Columbus, knowing an eclipse of the moon had been predicted for that night, told them that God would darken the moon unless they provided food. Hours later, as the eclipse began, the Tainos hurried to the ships with food, begging Columbus to pray to his God to save them.

Columbus also had to face a mutiny. In a pitched battle on May 19, 1504, watched by the Tainos, the mutineers were subdued and their leader was taken prisoner.

It is March 1504. Many months have passed, yet there is no sign of Méndez and Fieschi. Unknown to Columbus, they have reached Española, but Governor Ovando is in no hurry to rescue the Admiral.

An End and a Beginning

In June 1504 a rescue ship finally arrived. On August 13 Columbus sailed into Santo Domingo, which was now a thriving town. Ovando, the governor, greeted him with a show of affection. But it was, Fernando wrote, "the kiss of a scorpion."

In November Columbus returned to Spain, too ill to travel anymore. Shortly after, Queen Isabela died. Columbus spent his time petitioning Fernando to give him a tenth of the revenues from Española's mines as the sovereigns had promised. Columbus received only a fiftieth of the gold, but he was still a rich man when he died on May 20, 1506.

Columbus never reached Asia. He boasted and exaggerated, yet never succeeded in controlling the colony of which he was governor. The European animals and agricultural meth-

ods he and his men used brought great destruction to the local land. Worst of all, his "discoveries" led to the annihilation of the Tainos, whom he himself called gentle and harmless.

Yet Columbus's story is truly amazing. The son of an obscure Italian weaver, he captained the first European expedition to the Caribbean and the first to South America. Time after time he escaped death. His son Diego married into the Spanish royal family and, in 1509, sailed to Española as governor of the lands now called the West Indies.

Christopher Columbus's voyages helped shape the course of history. "To Spain," claimed a 16th-century writer, "Columbus gave a New World. History knows of no man who ever did the like."

On September 12, 1504, Columbus leaves Santo Domingo for Spain. Crippled with gout, he knows that he will never return.

How Do We Know?

There are many sources from which one can learn about Columbus, but it is important to know something about who wrote them, when, and why. Many sources are biased or limited in one way or another, and the historian must be careful in determining their accuracy.

PERSONAL ACCOUNTS

Columbus himself kept a record of his voyages. The original logbooks have been lost, but Bartolomé de Las Casas, the son of one of Columbus's men, copied the logs written during the first and third voyages. We know that Las Casas changed Columbus's text, but we do not know how much he changed it—did he just correct the grammar, or did he alter whole passages? Las Casas generally supported Columbus, so it is not surprising that in the logs the Admiral appears to be calm and masterful.

The log of the second voyage has disappeared completely. For evidence, we must rely on three accounts written by members of the crew. In these sources Columbus does not seem to be quite as good a leader as he does in his own logs.

Columbus never wrote an autobiography, but *The Book of Privileges, The Book of Prophecies,* and many of his letters have survived. In addition, Columbus's son Fernando wrote a biography of his father. Fernando was constantly trying to show that Columbus was in the right. By and large, he presents only information that supports his opinion. The only surviving account of the Talavera commission's report appears in his book. Historians use his account, but it is unlikely that a large commission of learned men would come to conclusions quite as foolish as those Fernando reports. Fernando sailed on the

fourth voyage, and it is interesting to compare his account of it, which he wrote much later, when he was 50 years old, with a letter that Columbus sent to the king and queen of Spain. Columbus is full of gloom, but Fernando's story is full of adventure and fun—perhaps because memory altered his perceptions.

OFFICIAL DOCUMENTS

After Columbus's death, his family tried to obtain the money due him from the government. Documents still exist from the court cases they brought to bear, but historians must remember that the statements made at

the hearings were all biased and were all made about 20 years after the events.

RESEARCH

Research continues to uncover new sources to help answer historians' questions. Alice B. Gould, one of the greatest researchers of Columbus, spent 20 years (1924–1944) searching through Spanish archives, tracking down the names of 87 of the 90 men who sailed on the first voyage. In addition, she found the original document in which Columbus says that he was born in Genoa.

The original had been missing because, during the Napoleonic Wars (1803–1815), the documents in the Spanish archives were used as bedding for cavalry horses and later jumbled together. Alice Gould sorted through hundreds of papers covered with dried manure until she found the original document.

Archaeologists also contribute to our knowledge of Columbus's story. For example, until recently historians believed that the fort at La Navidad was built next to the sea, but archaeologists have discovered that not only was it sited inland, in the middle of a Taino village, but also that it was never finished. In a nearby well were found the remains of a European pig and a rat's tooth. We know there were no rats in the Americas before the Spaniards arrived.

Researching the Taino and Carib peoples is especially difficult because they left no written records, and because the Spaniards destroyed nearly all of their treasures and possessions. Historians have to rely primarily on descriptions written by Spanish settlers, many of whom were prejudiced against the native peoples. Historians now think that the Spanish exaggerated tales of cannibalism, for example, to excuse the atrocities that they committed against the native peoples. A few Arawak Tainos still live in South America, but it is very difficult to determine how closely their culture resembles that of their ancestors.

STORIES AND MISCONCEPTIONS

Columbus is a controversial figure. In the Renaissance and in our own time, many people have praised him for his "discovery" of the New World, while many others have criticized him for being too religious or for obsessively seeking power and gold at the expense of the native inhabitants of the New World.

Along the way, stories and misconceptions have grown up about Columbus. Perhaps the most common misconception is that Columbus discovered North America — in fact, he never visited the present-day United States or Canada at all.

During his lifetime, Columbus's enemies spread rumors to harm his reputation. One such story claimed that he had been told about the New World by an "unknown navigator" who had come upon America by accident.

Columbus knew that people were criticizing him. In a letter describing the fourth voyage, he wrote about "those who find fault and scold, saying, 'Why did you not do something else?'" His response was simple. "I should have liked," he wrote, "to see *them* on this voyage."

Index

DUE DATE

MAY 17 1993		MAR 03 2014	
MAY 24 1993			
OCTOB 2 1993			
JUN 01 1994			
AUG 31 1994			
MAR. 01 1995			
FEB 03 96			
MAR 07 96			
OCT 23 97			
MAY 03 98			
OCT 24 99			
MAR 09 00			
DEC 16 2007			
APR 15 2009			
MAY 04 2011			
			Printed in USA

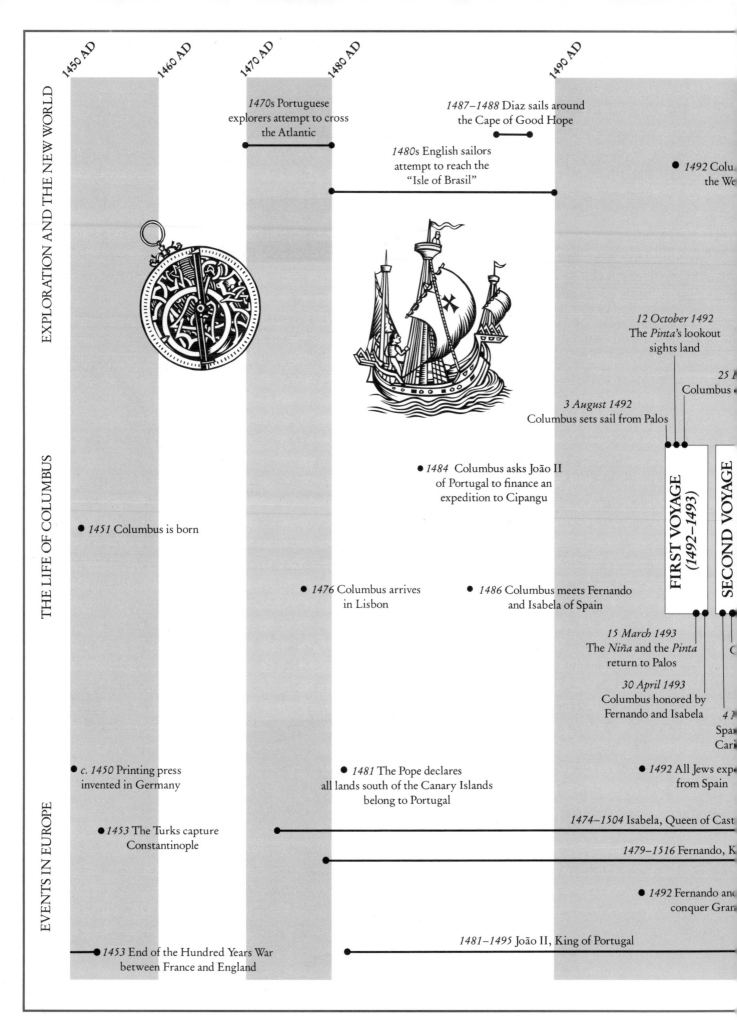

EXPLORATION AND THE NEW WORLD

1470s Portuguese explorers attempt to cross the Atlantic

1487–1488 Diaz sails around the Cape of Good Hope

1480s English sailors attempt to reach the "Isle of Brasil"

1492 Colu... the We...

THE LIFE OF COLUMBUS

12 October 1492
The *Pinta's* lookout sights land

*25 ...
Columbus ...*

3 August 1492
Columbus sets sail from Palos

● *1484* Columbus asks João II of Portugal to finance an expedition to Cipangu

● *1451* Columbus is born

FIRST VOYAGE (1492–1493)

SECOND VOYAGE

● *1476* Columbus arrives in Lisbon

● *1486* Columbus meets Fernando and Isabela of Spain

15 March 1493
The *Niña* and the *Pinta* return to Palos

30 April 1493
Columbus honored by Fernando and Isabela

*4 ...
Spa...
Cari...*

EVENTS IN EUROPE

● *c. 1450* Printing press invented in Germany

● *1481* The Pope declares all lands south of the Canary Islands belong to Portugal

● *1492* All Jews exp... from Spain

1474–1504 Isabela, Queen of Cast...

● *1453* The Turks capture Constantinople

1479–1516 Fernando, K...

● *1492* Fernando and conquer Gra...

1481–1495 João II, King of Portugal

1453 End of the Hundred Years War between France and England